TABLE OF CONTENTS

WHAT'S INSIDE?

Dinosaurs! These dinosaurs lived in cold places. Find out how they survived millions of years ago and what they have in common with today's animals.

LIFE IN COLD PLACES

Dinosaurs lived between 230 million and 65 million years ago. The world did not look the same then. The land and seas were not in the same places. Many dinosaurs lived near the north and south poles. It was very cold there.

CENTROSAURUS
AND OTHER DINOSAURS OF COLD PLACES

by Dougal Dixon

illustrated by
Steve Weston and James Field

PICTURE WINDOW BOOKS
Minneapolis, Minnesota

Picture Window Books
5115 Excelsior Boulevard
Suite 232
Minneapolis, MN 55416
877-845-8392
www.picturewindowbooks.com

Printed in the United States of America.

Library of Congress Cataloging-in-Publication Data
Dixon, Dougal.
Centrosaurus and other dinosaurs of cold places /
written by Dougal Dixon ; illustrations by James Field,
Steve Weston ; diagrams by Stefan Chabluk ; cover
art by Steve Weston.
p. cm. — (Dinosaur find)
Includes bibliographical references and index.
ISBN 1-4048-0672-5
1. Dinosaurs—Cold regions—Juvenile literature.
I. Field, James, 1959- ill. II. Weston, Steve, ill.
III. Chabluk, Stefan, ill. IV.
QE861.5.D364 2005
567.9—dc22

2004007305

Acknowledgments
This book was produced for Picture Window Books
by Bender Richardson White, U.K.

Illustrations by James Field (pages 4–5, 11, 13, 17, 21)
and Steve Weston (cover and pages 7, 9, 5, 19).
Diagrams by Stefan Chabluk.
All photographs copyright Digital Vision except page
16, Nigel J. Dennis: Gallo Images/Corbis Images Inc.

Consultant: John Stidworthy, Scientific Fellow
of the Zoological Society, London, and former
Lecturer in the Education Department, Natural
History Museum, London.

Reading Adviser: Rosemary G. Palmer, Ph.D.
Department of Literacy, College of Education,
Boise State University, Idaho.

Types of dinosaurs

In this book, a red shape at the
top of a left-hand page shows
the animal was a meat-eater.
A green shape shows it was
a plant-eater.

Just how big—or small—were they?

Dinosaurs were many different
sizes. We have compared their
size to one of the following:

Chicken
2 feet (60 cm) tall
Weight 6 pounds (2.7 kg)

Adult person
6 feet (1.8 m) tall
Weight 170 pounds (76.5 kg)

Elephant
10 feet (3 m) tall
Weight 12,000 pounds
(5,400 kg)

Many different dinosaurs wandered through the valleys. They were always hunting for food.

5

CENTROSAURUS

Pronunciation:
SEN-tro-SAW-rus

The *Centrosaurus* herd lived beside the lake all summer. Then the weather got colder. It was time for the herd to walk hundreds of miles. They set off to look for a place where food was still growing.

On the move today

Wildebeest travel in big herds to find new feeding grounds like *Centrosaurus* did millions of years ago.

Size Comparison

Young *Centrosaurus* marched in the middle of the herd. They were safer from enemies there.

CRYOLOPHOSAURUS

Pronunciation:
CRY-o-LO-fo-SAW-rus

Cryolophosaurus ate animals that it killed by itself. It also ate things that were already dead. Fish and dead sea creatures were sometimes washed on shore. Finding a meal was easier than catching it.

Showing off today

The cassowary that lives in Australia has a crest on its head like *Cryolophosaurus* once did.

Size Comparison

A *Cryolophosaurus* prowled along the cold shoreline. It would search through the sand and seaweed looking for a meal.

Edmontonia had a wide beak and lots of grinding teeth. It ground up tough needles and twigs from conifer trees. These were the only trees that grew in the far north.

Sharp weapons today

An elephant uses its tusks to frighten off enemies. *Edmontonia* used its spikes like this long ago.

Size Comparison

An *Edmontonia* would scare away meat-eaters. Its body was protected by spikes and armored plates on its back.

IGUANODON

Pronunciation:
ih-GWAN-o-dahn

Iguanodon did not find much to eat in winter. When it found food, it used its thumb spikes to tear down plants. It snipped off bites with its beak.

Thumb grips today

The giant panda uses its thumbs to grip plants like *Iguanodon* did.

Size Comparison

An *Iguanodon* wandered under the starry sky of winter. It left footprints in the sand.

13

Leaellynasaura had big eyes to see in the winter darkness. It had a beak for chewing tough leaves and ferns. Not many plants could be found during the long winter.

Big eyes today

Owls have big eyes to see in the dark like *Leaellynasaura* did millions of years ago.

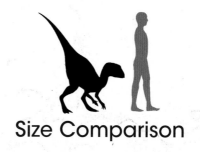

Size Comparison

In the darkness, a *Leaellynasaura* would peer beneath the frosty branches. There was not much food to be found.

15

Minmi could run well. It was also protected with armor. It had no head armor, but its underside was well protected. No other armored dinosaur had protection on its belly.

Protection today

A pangolin (scaly anteater) is covered with armor. It protects itself from enemies like *Minmi* once did.

Size Comparison

A *Minmi* crashed through the ice of a shallow pond to escape a large meat-eater.

17

Pachycephalosaurus had a bony dome on top of its head. It could have crashed its head into an enemy. Many meat-eaters would have backed away instead of fighting.

Head-on crash today

Male bison crash with their heads during fights like *Pachycephalosaurus* did long ago.

Size Comparison

A *Pachycephalosaurus* crashed its head into a *Tyrannosaurus*. It needed to keep the meat-eater away from its family.

TROODON

Pronunciation:
TROH-o-don

Troodon nested on the ground in cold, open country. It lived as a hunter. With its large eyes, it could see well. It was also a fast runner. *Troodon* had a big claw on its foot. It used it for killing animals to eat.

Family life today

Adult penguins sit on their eggs until they hatch like *Troodon* did millions of years ago.

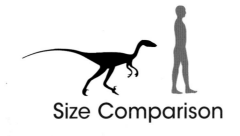

Size Comparison

The mother would sit on the eggs to keep them warm. The father would bring food to the mother so she didn't have to move.

21

WHERE DID THEY GO?

Dinosaurs are extinct, which means that none of them are alive today. Scientists study rocks and fossils to find clues about what happened to dinosaurs.

People have different explanations about what happened. Some people think a huge asteroid that hit Earth caused all sorts of climate changes. This then caused the dinosaurs to die. Others think volcanic eruptions caused the climate to change and that killed the dinosaurs. No one knows for sure, though.

Glossary

beak—the hard front part of the mouth of birds and some dinosaurs

ferns—plants with finely divided leaves known as fronds; ferns are common in damp woods and alongside rivers

grazes—eats low-growing plants; today's grazers eat grass and include sheep, goats, and cattle

hatch—to break out of an egg

herd—a large group of animals that move, feed, and sleep together

poles—ice-covered areas of Earth; the North Pole is known as the Arctic, and the South Pole as the Antarctic

shallow—not very deep

signaling—making a sign, warning, or hint

FIND OUT MORE

AT THE LIBRARY

Dispezio, Michael. *Dino Mania: Discovering Who's Who in the Jurassic Zoo.* New York: Sterling Publishing Co., 2002.

Dixon, Dougal. *Dinosaurs: Giants of the Earth.* Jackson, Tenn.: Davidson Titles, 1998.

Markle, Sandra. *Outside and Inside Dinosaurs.* New York: Atheneum Books, 2000.

ON THE WEB

FactHound offers a safe, fun way to find Web sites related to this book. All of the sites on FactHound have been researched by our staff.
www.facthound.com

1. Visit the FactHound home page.

2. Enter a search word related to this book, or type in this special code: 1404806725.

3. Click on the Fetch It button.

Your trusty FactHound will fetch the best Web sites for you!

INDEX